diatonic sequences for saxophone

from the music of j.s. bach

BACH SHAPES

by Jon De Lucia

MUSÆUM CLAUSUM PRESS

BROOKLYN, NY

*Thanks to Andrew Sterman, Sam Sadigursky, Dmitry Baevsky
and Tatsuya Sakurai for their invaluable input.*

Musæum Clausum Press
1117 8th Avenue #1RL
Brooklyn NY 11215

ISBN : 978-0-692-84477-9

Library of Congress Control Number: 2017902002

Book Design & Production: Chrissy Kurpeski

Music Composition & Layout: Jon De Lucia

TABLE OF CONTENTS

INTRODUCTION

This book came together as a result of my extended use of Bach and other baroque composers as a source of practice material and musical inspiration. I have used baroque materials to deal with many technical and musical issues and feel that much of it is applicable to the jazz player. It appears that many jazz players would agree. One has only to look at the work of John Lewis, Jacques Loussier, and Dave Brubeck, to name a few. This book is less about aesthetic crossover and more about deriving very flexible melodic material from the music of J.S. Bach. There have been numerous transcriptions of Bach's music for woodwinds, but in this book I wanted to distill the larger pieces into some of their major melodic components. This translates into a collection of diatonic sequences. I have done this with the intention that the improviser can then utilize these melodic shapes in their own spontaneous lines. The key word is spontaneous. Though these exercises have value when practiced methodically at home, the key is then to forget them and allow them to naturally occur in your improvising. Nothing is more deadly to real improvisation than mechanically running patterns through tunes on the bandstand. As the great Jimmy Giuffre said, "The music is you, and must always breathe fire. Never let it run straight and dry." Happy Practicing!

HOW TO PRACTICE

This book may be practiced in a variety of ways. While each exercise has been transposed into every key for you, it is worth learning to transpose these shapes on your own; the given examples are there to show you how. Ideally, one would spend a week or so with one pattern, learning how to play it the full range of the horn and through all twelve keys. If work is needed in one key in particular, focus on three or four exercises in one chapter. I have given one way to break down an exercise on the following page. You can also change notes, try to make the major shapes minor, or dominant. I have included a few exercises in the relative minor of each key, but these could easily be altered to become major key shapes. The key is to fully explore a shape that you like so that it becomes second nature and can organically surface in your playing. The shapes can easily be adapted to clarinet and flute as well. Regarding notes in the altissimo register, a lower option has been given if these notes are out of your range. There are no articulation markings given, but it is suggested that the exercises are played slurred first followed by any number of variations of tongued and slurred notes.

Embouchure Notes

It is crucial to have a relaxed but firm embouchure to play these exercises. You may have to take in more reed for the higher pitches, then less for the lower, but as Joe Allard says, do not drop the jaw. Strive for an "inclusive" embouchure that is relaxed enough to drop down large intervals but firm enough to reach high F. Practice the exercises slowly and check for evenness of sound and proper intonation, especially when approaching the altissimo notes.

A PRACTICAL EXAMPLE

Let's take a look at Exercise #9 in C Major.

It would be beneficial to isolate the first measure only, like this:

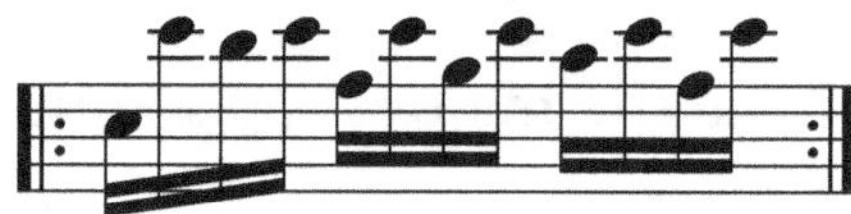

The widest interval here is the octave, C2 – C3.

Start by playing this interval, checking tuning and resonance. By resonance
I mean that you should be achieving the full tonal color of each note,
including a wide spectrum of overtones. If familiar with overtone practice,
check the C's against your low C overtone fingering and work to center your
sound before proceeding. More information on how to practice overtones
can be found in Sigurd Rascher's *Top Tones for the Saxophone* and Dave
Liebman's *Developing a Personal Saxophone Sound*. You will discover that you
may have to take in more reed as you go up the octave. This is preferable

to squeezing to ascend, or dropping the jaw to descend. A slight moving forward of lower lip along with a steady balance of firmness should achieve the intended sound.

Once your octave is established, maintain that feeling as you begin the exercise. The C's are your goalposts, to remain steady as you fill in the intervals between them. It may be beneficial to further break down the measure into 4-note groupings. Like this:

Other combinations are certainly possible. Practice all of the exercises slowly, considering these concepts until comfortable.

In terms of fingering difficulties, isolate any one particularly difficult interval and practice it at a steady tempo in the following rhythms, staying in any one measure until comfortable:

By breaking things down in this manner, one can find much to improve on in these exercises.

SOURCES OF BACH SHAPES

1. Violin Sonata No. 1 in G Minor BWV 1001

2. Flute Sonata No. 6 in E Major BWV 1035

3. Cello Suite No. 1 in G major BWV 1007

4. Violin Sonata No. 1 in G Minor BWV 1001

5. Violin Partita No. 2 in D Minor BWV 1004

6. Cello Suite No. 1 in G major BWV 1007

7. Violin Sonata No. 1 in G Minor BWV 1001

8. Violin Sonata No. 2 in A Minor BWV 1003

9. Invention No. 8 in F Major BWV 779

10. French Suite No. 2 in C Minor BWV 813

11. Violin Partita No. 2 in D Minor BWV 1004

12. Invention No. 8 in F Major BWV 779

13. Violin Sonata No. 1 in G Minor BWV 1001

14. Violin Partita No. 2 in D Minor BWV 1004

15. Violin Sonata No. 1 in G Minor BWV 1001

16. Violin Sonata No. 2 in A Minor BWV 1003

For Katie.

C Major

3.
4.
5.
6.
3

A Minor

— This page left intentionally blank. —

F Major

7.
8.
9.
10.

D Minor

— This page left intentionally blank. —

G Major

3.
4.
5.
6.

7.
8.
9.
10.
16   BACH SHAPES

E Minor

Bb Major

11. 
12. 
G Minor
13.

D Major

B Minor

14.

15.

16.

Eb Major

C Minor

A Major

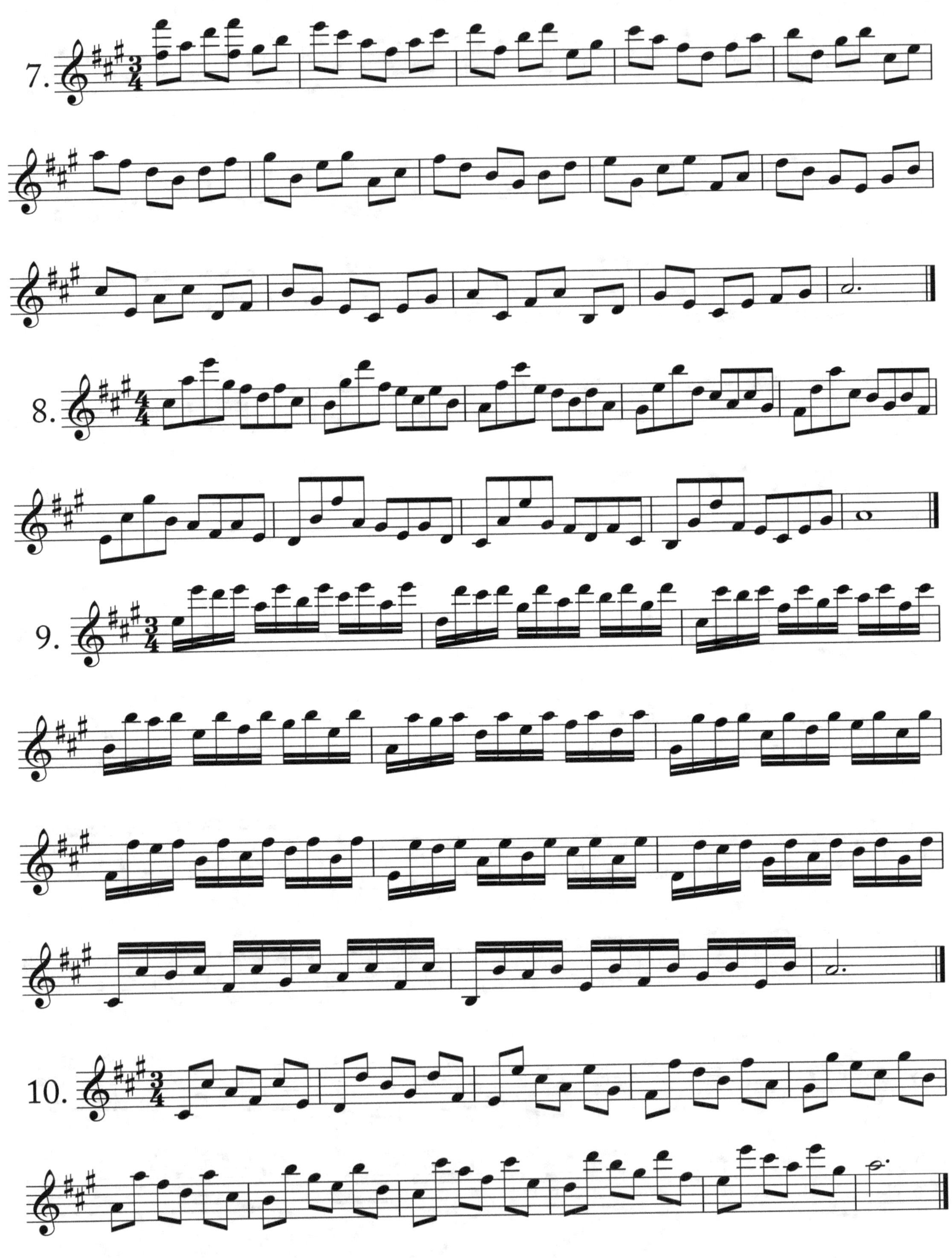

F# Minor

Ab Major

F Minor

E Major

C# Minor

Db Major

Bb Minor

B Major

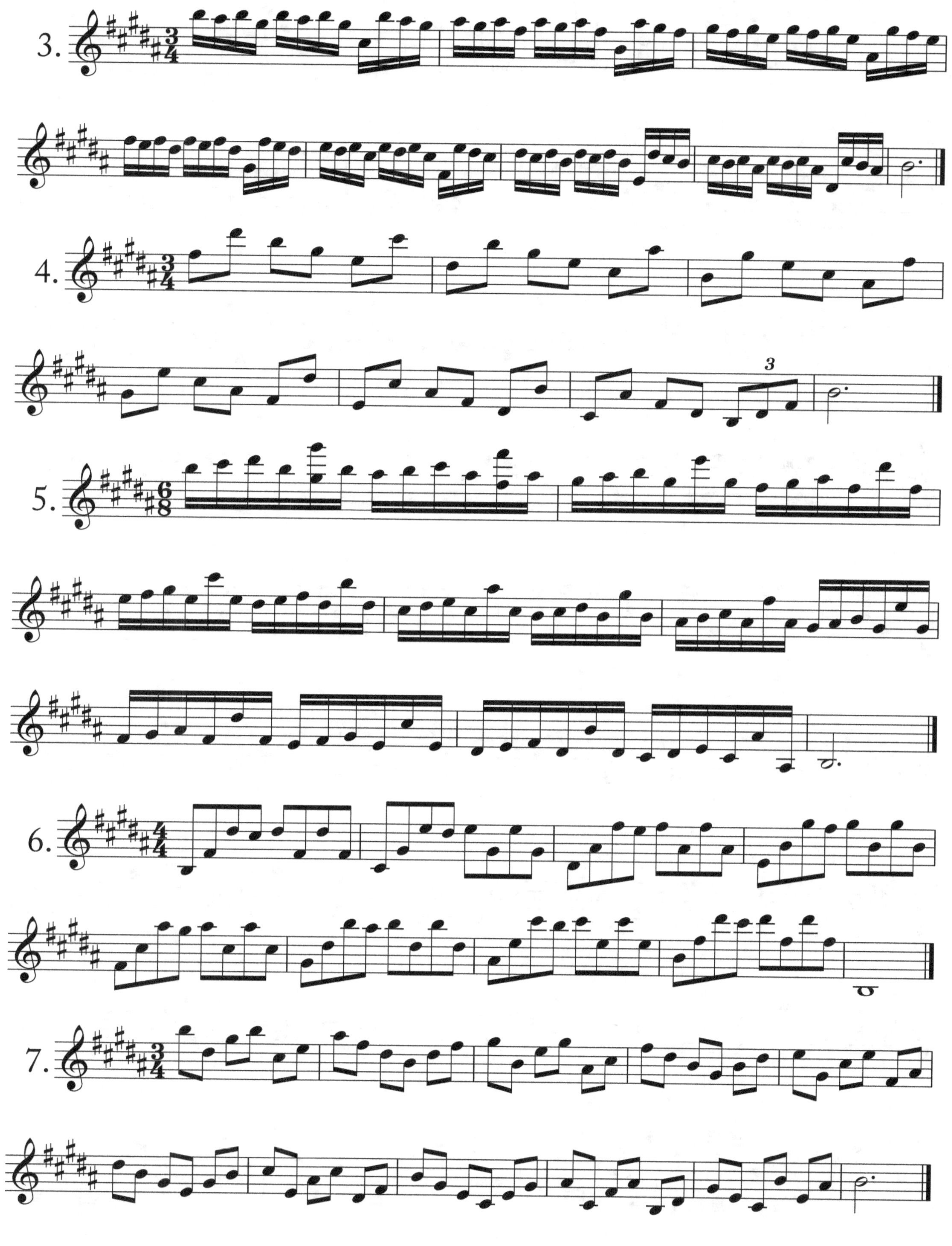

12. 
G# Minor
13.
BACH SHAPES 57

F# Major

11.
12.
D# Minor
13.

ETUDES

What follows are four etudes based on familiar standard progressions. The shapes are used freely here as motivic devices. The first etude is written as an exercise, while the remaining three are closer to improvised solos. Transposing and learning the etudes in another key is recommended to internalize the vocabulary.

Johann With The Wind

with shapes 5, 8, 11, 16

Just Freundes

with shapes 1, 2, 4, 5

Jon De Lucia

© Jon De Lucia Music

Bachground Music

with shapes 3, 4, 7, 9

Jon De Lucia

20,000 Fugues

with shapes 11, 12, 13, 14

Jon De Lucia

© Jon De Lucia Music